Hail the Gods

Pyrography of Idols of
Thor, Óðinn, and Freyja
by Jesseca Trainham

From the cover of the author's
Viking Poetry for Heathen Rites

Hail the Gods

Selections from
Viking Poetry for Heathen Rites

Eirik Westcoat

Skaldic Eagle Press
Long Branch, Pennsylvania
2019

Copyright © 2019 Eirik Westcoat

With proper attribution (for example, verbally or in a program booklet), the poems in this book may be freely read out loud (with or without minor changes) in not-for-profit religious rituals or poetry readings, whether private or public. All other rights reserved.

For permissions or other information,
please contact the author at
<eirik@theskaldiceagle.com>
or <www.theskaldiceagle.com>.

Cover art by Ermenegilda Muller
All layout and design by Eirik Westcoat

Collection of Winternights 2019

9 8 7 6 5 4 3 2 1

Paperback ISBN: 978-1-947407-10-7
Kindle Ebook ISBN: 978-1-947407-11-4

Skaldic Eagle Press
Long Branch, Pennsylvania

For the Aesir and Vanir

Acknowledgements

All poems contained in this volume were previously published in my *Viking Poetry for Heathen Rites*. Before that, "Öfundarmál," "A Tale of Wisdom's Well," and "Valhalla" were published in issues of *Idunna* by The Troth.

The poem "Eirik's Hymn" is a loose translation and heathen reinterpretation of the Old English "Cædmon's Hymn."

The frontispiece image by Jesseca Trainham first appeared on the front cover of my *Viking Poetry for Heathen Rites* in 2017 and is used here with permission.

Special thanks go to Ermenegilda Muller for her striking and intricate cover art for this volume.

Table of Contents

Preface viii
Eirik's Hymn 1
Heathen Pride 2
Nine Noble Virtues 4
Perseverance 7
The Binding of Fenrir 9
The Brísingamen 12
Building Asgard's Wall 18
The Duel 21
Freyr and Gerð 26
Gunnlaðarljóð 27
Iðunn's Abduction 30
The Mead Quest 34
The Six Treasures 36
Thor's Visit to Geirröð 38
Valhalla 42
A Drápa for Formal Sumbel 45
Fólksdrápa 49
Pagan Praise to Freyr 53
Thor Processional Chant 56
An Ull Poem 59
Sumartímadrápa 60
Vetrartímadrápa 63
A Yule Poem 66
Öfundarmál 67
A Tale of Wisdom's Well 70
Yggdrasilsdrápa 72
Rise and Reach the Gods! 77

Preface

Even as I prepared my first book, *Viking Poetry for Heathen Rites*, I knew it was a "grand gesture" of a sort, and that its size and price might be a bit intimidating to some prospective readers. However, the poems insisted — absolutely insisted — upon this.

Thus, I honored the poems' wishes by putting them in a comprehensive collection of liturgical poems for hallowing space, telling stories from the mythology, inviting the holy powers to blessings, staging ritual dramas, praying, and praising the gods. That book aimed for completeness.

Now, however, I feel that it is time for many of those poems (primarily from two of those categories, telling stories from the mythology and praising the gods) to reach a wider audience in a different format — a format that is more along the lines of what comes to mind when a typical reader thinks of a poetry book. So here they are, in a light, delicate, and friendly little volume. This book aims for focus and enjoyment.

If you do not already have my *Viking Poetry for Heathen Rites* — and I assume most buying this book will not — I hope it will inspire you with the possibilities for bringing the old gods and old ways to today's world.

Winternights 2019
Eirik Westcoat

Eirik's Hymn

Heimdall we praise, Heaven's Warder,
and measuring Týr's might and wisdom
and Woden's works of wondrous glory —
that Eternal Drighten from time's beginning.
The worlds were shaped for shining offspring
with heaven as a roof by that Holy Ruler.
Midgard he made, Mankind's Patron,
and that Eternal Drighten truly adorned
the earth with Men for Ingvi's blessings.

Heathen Pride

We are hearty heathens,
happy and proud;
the gods of the North
we gladly hail.
The honored ancestors'
awesome gods
are kith and kin
and keep us together.

We eagerly learn
the elder lore
and the needful virtues
of noble ancestors.
Óðinn of the Aesir
we honor for wisdom,
the power of poetry,
and the potent Runes.

Týr the one-handed
— the Wolf he bound —
we honor for courage
and order in the world.
Thor we hail
for hammer of might;
he wards and hallows
our holy steads.

Freyja for freedom
and frolic we hail;
her love and pleasure
lifts our spirits.
Freyr we hail
for harvest's reward
and peace and plenty
in proper seasons.

Many more
of mighty gods
we bid and hail
in holy blessings.
In raising our horns
with holy mead,
we hail heathenry
and heathen pride!

Nine Noble Virtues

Virtues I name,
nine in all;
hallowed by heathens,
they help your life.
Noble and needful,
know them well;
prudent and powerful,
practice them well.

The first I know,
its name is Truth.
Awesome Óðinn
is always seeking it.
A path to power,
pleasure, and wisdom —
it is dear to dolts
and drightens alike.

The second I know,
its name is Self-Reliance.
If wandering the world,
your way to make,
or hallowing your home
to hold in prosperity,
have strength inside
to steer your course.

The third I know,
its name is Discipline.
Know when on the path
to peer around,
and when in the hall
to hold your tongue,
and when to act,
awesome in might.

The fourth I know,
its name is Industriousness.
Always rise early
if you aim for wealth
and mindful be
of meetly deeds,
working hard
for the hope of Jera.

The fifth I know,
its name is Perseverance.
Óðinn did hang,
eagerly on the Tree;
through nine of nights
he never quit.
Endurance obtained
the dear-bought Runes.

The sixth I know,
its name is Courage.
Hold to right
though harm may come.
Bloodthirsty Fenrir
was bound by Týr.
He lost his hand,
but hale was his soul.

The seventh I know,
its name is Fidelity.
Have fullness of faith
in friends who are true
and to ginn-holy gods
be gracious always,
choosing often
to exchange with both.

The eighth I know,
its name is Hospitality.
The self-serving ale
Aegir provided,
and his good attendants
were greatly praised;
gold in that hall
was glowing for light.

The ninth I know,
its name is Honor.
To self be true
and tread with right,
willingly keep
your words of pledge,
and in thoughts and words
and works accord.

Virtues I've named,
nine in all.
Rede they give
if rede you need.
Useful if used,
use them well,
and a hallowed name
among heathens you'll earn.

Perseverance

Perseverance
is a powerful virtue.
Steadfast in struggles
you should strive to be
— resolute and firm
if facing hardship —
to succeed and prevail
in seeking victory.

Óðinn did hang
eagerly on the Tree;
through nine of nights,
he never quit;
wounded and hungry,
he willed to succeed.
Endurance obtained
the dear-bought Runes.

Óðinn went seeking
Óðrœrir's poetry;
the labor of slaves
for a long summer
had bought Bölverk
Baugi's favor.
He pilfered that mead
with patient work.

Geirröð abused
Grímnir with fire;
for eight of nights
the agony continued
'til Agnarr gave
Óðinn a drink.
Strength of commitment
had made him stay.

Gleipnir's getter
had gained for Freyr
glorious Gerð,
Gymir's daughter;
Skírnir endured,
undaunted by threats.
Tenacity fulfilled
that needful errand.

Gored upon spears,
Gullveig was burned;
that witch endured
the worst of pain
'til reborn as Heið,
bright and holy.
Unwavering purpose
won that victory.

If faced with need
and fearsome toil,
remember that Ash,
awesome in might;
though heavily oppressed,
it holds its place.
Strong you must be,
steadfast like that Tree.

The Binding of Fenrir

The ale of Ygg
I eagerly brewed,
and here I pour that poem.
Of Fenrir's binding
and famous Týr,
that spell I speak to all.

Loki and Angrboða,
they lay together
and a gruesome three they begat.
A woman half-corpse,
a wolf, and a serpent:
these offspring were destined for doom.

The wolf alone
waxed in Asgard,
fed by trusty Týr.
But fast he grew
and was greatly feared;
the Aesir sought an answer.

Fenrir they chose
to fetter and bind,
to save their home from harm.
They bid him try
and test his strength
against the chains they chose.

With a mighty thrash,
he threw off Leyðing:
that fetter failed to hold!
With a mighty strain,
he struck off Drómi:
that fetter failed to hold!

Freyr's friend,
fair Skírnir,
from dwarves he fetched a fetter.
Subtle runes,
six in all,
were blended to form that bond:

woman's beard,
bear's sinews,
mountain's mighty roots,
fish's breath,
bird's spittle,
and cat's noise of falling feet.

Soft and smooth
like a silken ribbon,
yet firm and fast as well:
the Aesir wished
the wolf to try
Gleipnir against his strength.

The wolf had guessed
that guile and tricks
were used to form that fetter;
a pledge as proof
to place in his mouth,
he demanded from the mighty Aesir.

And almost all
the Aesir refused
to pledge the price required,
but honorable Týr
offered his hand,
the weregild the wolf desired.

With the slender band,
they bound the wolf:
that fetter firmly held!
But the wolf's price
was paid by Týr:
in lying he lost his hand.

On Lyngvi Isle
in Lake Amsvartnir,
Fenrir is firmly held
with Gleipnir by Gelgja
on Gjöll attached,
thrust by Thviti in ground.

A mighty sword
in his mouth is thrust;
that burden stops his bite.
Howling horribly,
Hope from his mouth
runs as a river of spit.

Fast today
that fetter holds,
and ever after still,
until that day
of terrible dark:
the time of Ragnarök.

The Brísingamen

Might with metals
is the main of dwarves,
and as good as any
are Grérr, Álfrigg,
Dvalinn, and Berling
in doing that work.
In a rock they lived
and wrought their craft.

Word of their work
had wended far,
flying to Asgard
and Freyja's ears.
In a day of wandering,
the Dís of the Vanir
came in the cave
of these crafty dwarves.

The eyes of Freyja
then angled upon
a gleaming necklace
of gold and amber.
'Twas Brísingamen,
the best of jewels,
and Fólkvang's lady
was flaming with lust.

The greatest treasure
of gold and silver
she offered to them
to own that jewel.
But the dwarves declined
and deemed her money
a rather poor price
for parting with it.

The craftsmen then
declared their price:
her body would be
the best exchange.
In love and lust
she'd lay with them
for one night each
to win that jewel.

For nights all four,
her nubile form
sated the lust
of salacious dwarves;
furtively then
Freyja returned,
back to her bower
with the beautiful jewel.

But Loki had witnessed
that long exchange
of carnal delights,
craving mischief.
As with Sif before,
he would seek a way
to slip inside
and seize her treasure.

Alone at night,
Loki then searched.
In form of fly
he flitted around,
hoping to find
a hole to enter.
Up by the gable
he gained his entrance.

Freyja was found
by Farbauti's son,
soundly sleeping
inside her bower.
Above her breast
was Brísingamen;
beneath her neck
was the needed clasp.

Into form of flea
the feisty one
then changed and bit
her cheek with malice.
Startled she stirred,
then stretched and turned.
The clasp exposed,
he carried it off.

When morning came,
Mardöll awoke
and noticed now
her necklace gone.
Unbroken but open
was her bower door.
Was it Byleist's brother
who'd been inside?

To the hall of Hár
she hastened for news,
asking if any
had answers to give.
Where was Loki
or the winsome jewel?
The gathered Aesir
together mooted.

The sly one was seen
sneaking away,
carrying something
he was keeping hidden.
Whither went he
wending quickly?
Silent Víðarr
to Singasteinn pointed.

On hearing that news,
Heimdall the White
stood and started
and stammered almost.
As warden of Bifröst
he watches the realms,
yet mischief's maker
he'd missed completely.

The son of sisters
then sought to redeem
his failure of sight
by finding the thief.
Great Gullintanni
would regain that jewel,
his service pledged
to Sýr for honor.

Valiant Vindlér
ventured to Singasteinn,
a skerry far out
and scoured by winds.
To reach that rock,
from radiant Ull
he received a bone
to surf the waves.

A seal was swimming
in the sea nearby,
splashing around
in sparkling water.
A shape-shifter
he'd surely found,
Sýr's servant knew,
on seeing its eyes.

The burly brute
then barked in anger
when he realized
the watchman saw him.
Under the waves
he went and vanished,
leaving Heimdall
alone on the rock.

But Heimdall was skilled
in the hidden magics
and knew the charms
to change his shape.
He rowned some runes
in a rhythmic chant;
to shape of seal
he shifted his form.

In the drink he dove,
down after the fiend,
flapping flippers
in furious pursuit.
The warrior warden
in water moved quick
and nearly caught
crafty Nálarson.

Loki evaded
and leapt on the rock
to face and fight
his furious pursuer.
The bouncing blubbers
in battle then crashed,
a serious struggle
on Singasteinn.

Heimdall with his head
then hammered Loki.
It served him well
as a sword of might,
for the top of his tree,
containing authority,
availed against Loki
for victory on the rock.

Byleist's brother
was beat at last;
regained for Gefn
was the gleaming jewel.
Loki was bound
and led back home.
Heimdall's honor
was healed through glory.

Now that necklace
is on noble Freyja;
it brightens her beauty,
that best of jewels,
for Mardöll is honored
by mighty treasures,
that glorious mother
of Gersemi and Hnoss.

Building Asgard's Wall

Silence I seek
for saying my tale
of the master mason
who meant to build
for the garth of the Gods
the greatest of walls;
with Ygg's ale now
I utter my words.

Midgard was made
and mighty Valhöll;
for proof against
the passage of etins,
the Aesir sought
a solid defense;
a builder offered
the best of walls.

The sun and moon
he sought as payment
and Freyja to wed
as fairest wife;
the Aesir allowed
only a winter —
if unfinished the fort,
then forfeit his wage.

Alone must he labor,
allowed no help;
an exception he sought
— Svaðilfari his horse —
and Loki arranged
that the right be granted.
With winter's start
the work was begun.

The stallion's work
startled the gods;
he steadily hauled
the heavy stones
— always at night —
and every day
the builder labored
to lay the wall.

Fast proceeded
the fort's assembly;
by summer's start
it would stand complete.
The Aesir assembled
on seats of judgement
to moot on their doom
and deem a response.

It was soon decided
that the son of Laufey
should bear the blame
for the blight approaching.
Thus Loki must manage
that the mason forfeit,
or Lopt would lose
his life for failing.

When evening came,
out ran a mare
who neighed to distract
the stallion from work.
Away he wended
towards the mare
with the hapless builder
hurrying after.

The chase continued,
taking all night;
the stallion's running
had stopped the work.
With day's dawning
deduced the mason
that for certain his fee
forfeit would be.

The mason raged
with wrath of etins
for all to see.
The Aesir summoned
Thor from the East
to thrash the etin —
with Mjöllnir's power
he paid his wage.

But Svaðilfari had sated
himself on Loki,
and some time after,
Sleipnir was born.
Eight-footed and grey,
an awesome steed —
amongst the gods
and men the best.

The Duel

For saying my tale
of single combat
at Grjóttúnagarðar,
a gift of silence
I ask from you all.
To utter my story,
I brewed my words
into Bölverk's wine.

On swift Sleipnir
had Sigföður rode;
Hrungnir he met
in the home of Etins.
Óðinn boasted
that best was Sleipnir;
Hrungnir disputed,
praising Gullfaxi.

In anger he galloped;
Óðinn he chased.
Fast he traveled
and before he knew,
the gates of the gods
he'd galloped through,
but Sleipnir was still
the swifter steed.

The Aesir bade
that burly Hrungnir
enter the hall
and have a drink.
The goblets of Thor
were given to him;
dead drunk he got,
draining each one.

With big words then
he boasted loudly:
that hall he would take
to the home of Etins.
Then he'd sink Asgard
and slay the gods
— except he'd filch
Sif and Freyja.

Only Freyja
would fetch him drink,
and all the ale
of the Aesir he'd have,
but bored of boasting,
the band of gods
then hailed to Thor
who thundered in.

He threatened Hrungnir
with hammer raised,
in spite of Óðinn's
offer of safety.
Hrungnir challenged
Hlórriði to duel
at Grjóttúnagarðar
for greater honor.

Thor accepted
the summons and spared
the unarmed etin
an honorless death,
for never before
had formal duel
been offered thus
to Eindriði.

At Grjóttúnagarðar
gathered the Etins.
To serve Hrungnir
as second in battle,
they made from clay
Mökkurkálfi —
enormously high
with heart of mare.

But Hrungnir had
a heart of stone;
of hard stone also
his head was made.
His shield and weapon
were shaped from stone;
his spleen as well
was spawned of rocks.

But prior to Thor,
Thjálfi arrived.
He advised the etin
that from underground
Véurr was advancing
to avoid his shield;
on the wheel of Hild,
Hrungnir then stood.

Water was made
by Mökkurkálfi
when furious Thor
in thunder appeared.
The clay coward
was killed by Thjálfi
with little of fight
and less of fame.

Arriving in rage,
Rym then quickly
hurled his hammer
at Hrungnir's bulk;
his whetstone-weapon
he whirled in return,
but through the hone
the hammer smashed.

The rock ruptured,
rammed by Mjöllnir;
into Hlórriði's head
then hied a shard.
The other fragment
fell to the earth
and became the world's
whetstone supply.

Into Hrungnir's head
the hammer continued
and smashed asunder
his source of thoughts.
Forward he fell,
fettering Sönnung;
firmly his feet
made fast that god.

Thjálfi and the Aesir
to Thor then came;
the limbs of the troll
they tried to lift.
But the heavy bulk
of Hrungnir's body
remained immobile
'til Magni arrived.

Though three years old,
the Ása-strength
of Jörð's grandson
— Járnsaxa's boy —
quickly lifted
those legs of stone;
he got Gullfaxi
as a gift from Thor.

Stuck in Thor's head
the stone remains,
though loosened a little
by the lays of Gróa;
By news of Aurvandil's
nearing to home
and his toe as a star,
he distracted her spells.

The stone that's stuck
still has an effect —
thus it is ill
that over the ground
you throw a hone,
for in Thor's head then
the stone is stirred,
distressing Ennilang.

Savor these sips
of sweetest mead,
and remember well
in mind this tale
of Vingþórr's victory
in valiant combat
at Grjóttúnagarðar,
the greatest of duels!

Freyr and Gerð

Freyr, from Hliðskjálf,
saw the fairest of maidens:
beautiful Gerð in her garth.
He sank into sorrow,
sore with longing,
heavy with heartache for the maid.

Skírnir he sent
to score her love,
yearning for the jötunn maid.
Enticing with Draupnir,
then tempting with apples,
the messenger sought that match.

The gifts she refused,
then great was his wrath:
with self-swinging sword he menaced.
But finally with threats
of thurs-runes carved,
the maiden agreed to marriage.

Both then in tryst
at Barri were wedded;
Freyr and Gerð are together.
Our joyous Lord
has rejoined the world
with a heart that's whole again.

Gunnlaðarljóð

Home at Hnitbjörg,
a hall in a mountain,
the daughter of Suttung dwelled.
Gorgeous Gunnlöð
was guarding his mead,
that 'gild from dwarves he gained.

Suttung savored
for himself alone
the precious and potent mead,
though that sumbel sat
unsipped by all
in a room so deep and dark.

Gunnlöð sat
on her golden stool
and dreamed of worlds all-wide.
Tales of heroes:
from travelers she heard
those stories of might and main.

She hoped that a hero
would hie for the mead
and relieve her lonely days.
Well she knew
that the wondrous brew
had a better and brighter wyrd.

By stone grinding
she was startled one day
from her bed of brooding dreams.
A hole appeared
in the hardened wall;
was it the hoped-for hero?

With bated breath,
from her bed she rose
as a serpent slithered out.
Before her eyes
its form had altered
to the Ás she knew was Óðinn!

Óðinn asked
to earn the mead
that Gunnlöð guarded there.
Her lust inflamed,
she allowed to him
her help to win that wine.

Secured it was
by crafty spells
and powerful chants and charms.
Galdor they'd need
to gain its release
and thus keep Hár from harm.

Sexual seið
and sorcery they worked,
grinding together with lust.
Nights all three
they needed to finish
the magic to ready the mead.

Their working done,
they wended then
to the cauldrons keeping the mead.
Óðinn sat
in eager suspense
on the stool of glowing gold.

Gunnlöð gave
to Gaut Óðrœrir,
then Boðn and Són to swig.
In sorrow she served
those sips of mead,
for she knew he'd not return.

Grímnir altered
to glorious eagle
and soared in searing sky,
leaving Gunnlöð
alone to grieve
for the hero she helped and loved.

Iðunn's Abduction

For the ale of Óðinn
I eagerly quested;
I won that potion
and well I pour it.
Of Iðunn's abduction
I aim to tell
and her return to home
and what happened after.

Hœnir and Loki
were hiking with Óðinn
across the wastelands
and wilderness paths;
the hungry gods:
from a herd they took
and in earth oven
an ox they would cook.

But uncooked the ox
in the oven remained
when once and twice
they tested the meat.
Their supper delayed,
they sought a reason
and an eagle they heard
in the oak above.

The eagle demanded
the meat of his choice
for allowing the oven
at last to cook.
The Aesir agreed,
and the greedy eagle
ate the shoulders
and also the hams.

The eagle was attacked
by angry Loki.
He struck with a stick
but it stuck in place
against the eagle
when up it flew;
he was carried away,
crying for truce.

Loki agreed,
to gain his freedom,
to lure Iðunn
with her apples alone,
outside the walls
away from Asgard;
thus Loki at last
was released by the eagle.

Then Loki lured
lovely Iðunn
just as promised
to giant's grasp;
both old and grey
the gods became,
lacking her famous
and luscious fruit.

The Aesir accused
crafty Loki
and deemed the penalty
death or torture;
he'd search for Iðunn
to save his skin
if Freyja would share
her falcon shape.

To Thjazi's home
hastened Loki.
Laufeyson was lucky;
its lord was away.
The falcon flew
with the form of a nut,
Iðunn bespelled,
as he sped away.

The theft was discovered
when Thjazi returned;
the issue of Ölvaldi
as eagle gave chase.
The falcon flew
fast to Asgard
and reached the safety
inside its walls.

The eagle was unable
to end its flight,
its feathers singed
by sawdust's fire.
The eagle crashed
in the Aesir's court,
and quickly was slain
the sire of Skaði.

Then Skaði with weapons
wended to Asgard,
thirsting for vengeance
for Thjazi her father,
but an offer of weregild
the Aesir made,
and atonements three
she took from the gods.

First for Skaði:
to find a husband,
from the Aesir she'd choose,
but only by feet.
The fairest of feet
she figured for Baldur,
but Njörð she got,
Nóatún's lord.

Second for Skaði:
skillful Loki,
by binding his balls
to the beard of a goat,
looked to release
a laugh from her heart;
he fell in her lap
and at last it was freed.

Third for Skaði:
that in sky above
shaped into stars,
shining at night,
the eyes of Thjazi
were thrown by Óðinn —
for her fierce father,
the finest honor.

With atonements three
was Thjazi's daughter
with the ruling Regin
reconciled and joined.
Thus Skaði we honor
for skis and snow
and wild winter's
wondrous delights.

The Mead Quest

Honor I Óðinn
by eagerly pouring
that precious and potent Mead.
How he won
that wynnful draught —
that spell I speak in verse.

Slaves all nine
were slain with greed
in lust for a worthy whetstone.
Thus Bölverk served
Baugi a summer;
he labored long and hard.

Bölverk had bargained
with Baugi for Mead;
at Hnitbjörg his hire they sought.
But flatly Suttung
refused that draught;
to a skillful scheme they turned.

Baugi with Rati
then bored through rock
and gnawed a narrow path.
The sly snake
then slithered fast
beyond his stinging stab.

Gunnlöð he met
and gained her love;
for three of nights he knew her.
The draughts he drank
and drained were three —
that mighty Mead he stole.

The eagle flew
to Asgard fast
with Suttung swiftly chasing.
An amount of Mead
as mud of eagle
for poetry poor was spilt.

But the greatest bounty
he brought to the gods —
a gift for the favored few.
Óðinn poured
that potent brew
for skalds and scholars alike.

For Man in Midgard
the Mead is real:
seek to win it yourself.
Drink well
and deeply enjoy
the portion I poured tonight!

The Six Treasures

Bölverk's bounty
I bear tonight
and pour a portion to share.
I tell a tale
of treasures six,
owned by our awesome gods.

The beautiful locks
of alluring Sif
were sheared by mischief's maker;
Thor was wroth,
raged at Loki,
demanded he find a fix!

Then Loki wended
to the world of Dwarves;
their skill he schemed to hire.
The smiths began,
the sons of Ívaldi:
Goldlocks they gleamingly shaped.

The smiths continued,
the sons of Ívaldi:
Skíðblaðnir they skillfully shaped.
The smiths finished,
the sons of Ívaldi:
Gungnir they grimly shaped.

Then Loki wended
to wager with Brokk
against the greatness of treasures.
A swine's skin
by skillful Eitri
was forged to gleaming Gullinbursti.

Glowing gold
by gifted Eitri
was forged to dearest Draupnir.
Blazing iron
by brilliant Eitri
was forged to foe of etins,
was forged to mighty Mjöllnir.

Brokk was steady,
on bellows he stayed,
the scheme of the fly he foiled!
Treasures he took
to try in Asgard,
Aesir joining in judgement.

Óðinn and Thor,
and third was Freyr,
the gods who joined in judgement.
The given verdict,
the greatest treasure:
best was bane of etins,
best was mighty Mjöllnir!

Thor's Visit to Geirröð

A warm welcome
I wish to have
for telling the tale
of a trip by Thor
to Geirröð's garth
and the games in the hall;
the draught of dwarves
I draw for you now.

Loki borrowed
from Lady Frigg
her falcon shape
to fly the realms;
at Geirröð's garth
a great hall was —
Lopt then landed
and looked in the window.

Geirröð ordered
they grab the bird;
Loki delayed
to the last moment
his flight to flee
that fellow's grasp
but found his feet
were firmly stuck.

The bird was bound
and brought to Geirröð;
on seeing the eyes,
an inkling he had
that a man it be.
He demanded the bird
speak in response;
speechless was Loki.

The unanswered etin
opened a chest
and brutally bound
the bird inside
for three of months
to thirst and starve.
Re-asked at last,
Loki then answered.

To ransom his life,
Loki gave oaths:
to Geirröð's garth
he'd beguile Thor,
without Mjöllnir
and mighty girdle.
Released was Loki
to lure as promised.

To Gríð's garth first
as a guest came Thor;
she gave warning
of Geirröð's wiles.
Iron gauntlets,
a girdle of might,
and Gríðarvöl
she gave as well.

To cross Vimur
then ventured Thor;
the river raged,
rising in flood
with Gjálp astride,
Geirröð's daughter.
Thor was struggling
but threw a stone.

He did not miss
the mark he aimed;
the stone then stemmed
and stopped the source.
He grasped a rowan
by river's edge;
thus it is hight
the help of Thor.

Thor and Loki
at last arrived
at Geirröð's garth
and were given lodging.
The single seat there
Sönnung did take;
toward the roof
it raised him up.

With Gríðarvöl
against the rafters
and pushing hard,
he pressed down then;
Both Gjálp and Greip
— Geirröð's daughters —
had their backs broken
for bearing the seat.

For games in the hall,
Geirröð called Thor
and threw a measure
of molten iron
at famous Véurr,
the friend of Man.
Eindriði caught
the iron with gloves.

The etin sought shelter
from an iron pillar;
but briskly Thor
flung back the lump.
It passed through the pillar,
plunged through Geirröð,
soared through the wall,
and sank in the earth.

Here in Midgard,
remember this tale
— with precious Óðrœrir
I poured it out —
for the evil of etins
on earth is lessened
by victorious Véurr's
valor in combat.

Valhalla

A spell of the lore
I speak to you now
by pouring Hropt's
powerful drink.
I sing of that hall
high on the Tree;
to warriors dead
'tis a welcome sight.

'Tis roofed with shields
and raftered with spears;
grand and glorious
in Glaðsheim stands
that greatest hall
of gods and heroes
where sturdy benches
are strewn with mail.

A wolf is lurking
at the western door,
and high above
hovers an eagle.
Fish are running
in the river nearby;
mistletoe's in the west,
a mite of a tree.

The leaves are eaten
from Læráð by Heiðrún;
mead from her udders
is the Einherjar's drink.
The limbs are eaten
from Læráð by Eikþyrnir;
dew from his horns
drops into Hvergelmir.

The gate Valgrind
is guarding the doors:
five of hundreds
and forty more.
The Einherjar go,
eight hundred per door,
on the day of doom
for deadly battle.

In the kettle Eldhrímnir,
the cook Andhrímnir
seethes Sæhrímnir,
that succulent pork.
The Einherjar eat
that excellent fare,
but the food of Vegtam
is fed to his wolves.

The wise one lives
on wine alone;
his ravens fly,
roaming the world.
The Valkyries serve
Victory-Father
and after the battles
the Einherjar's feasting.

Bragi relates
lore to Aegir;
swords shimmering
are the source of light.
Sigmund and Sinfjötli
receive the guests;
from fields of battle,
fresh they arrive.

Hrungnir challenged
Hlórriði to duel;
he dared to boast,
drunk in that hall.
Glasir gleaming
with golden leaf
is standing in front
of the famous stead.

That hall is sought
by heroes and skalds;
both far and wide
its fame has spread.
Standing strongest,
that stead is best:
it is Óðinn's own,
awesome Valhalla!

A Drápa for Formal Sumbel

In quest I struggled
to quicken my words
and honor Óðinn tonight;
The drink of dwarves:
that draught I won,
and now I pour it in praise.

Hail to Óðinn,
the Aesir's lord
and greatest worker of wode.
The raven god
has roamed the worlds
and waxed in wisdom's might.

This god of heroes
is the greatest hero,
for the best of the Aesir is Óðinn.

He hung wounded
on that holy tree
to gain the glorious Runes;
with the price he paid
of pain and torment
were might and mystery won!

He is always seeking
to add to his wisdom,
for the best of the Aesir is Óðinn.

Suttung's sumbel
he sought to steal
to gain the skill of skalds;
by knowing Gunnlöð
for nights all three
were power and poetry won!

The Folk in Midgard
is fortunate indeed
to share in those greatest of gains;
for winning the Runes
and winning the Mead,
hail to the heroes' god,
hail to awesome Óðinn!

Now I turn
my needful praise
to the heroes in Óðinn's hall;
With mead I toast
those mighty dead
who eternally fight and feast.

Hail to the Einherjar,
the heroes of Óðinn,
those champions chosen in battle;
they feast in Valhöll
with the father of victory
on the best of boar and mead.

The cream of the Folk
is called for that host;
the honor of the Einherjar is eternal.

The greatest of warriors
have gained that hall
by trusting in might and main.
Their deeds and doings
of daring in battle
inspire our spirits today.

With glory in Glaðsheim,
together they dwell;
the honor of the Einherjar is eternal.

The greatest of skalds
have gained that hall
through pouring their mighty mead.
In the workings of Wyrd
their words live on:
the great reward for wode.

The lives they lived
are a light to heathens;
their glory is undying in death.
For showing the way
to that shining hall,
hail to the Heroes of the Folk,
hail to Óðinn's Einherjar!

To the Folk's future,
forward I look
and praise the past as well;
A full horn I raise
to the Folk today —
the modern heathen heroes.

Hail to the Folk
of heathen faith
who struggle to restore that troth!
We aim to emulate
the Einherjar well
through our mighty words and works.

Our local kindreds
labor with pride;
the fame of our Folk is growing.

To the chiefs and elders
who've chosen to lead
and bear that burden well,
and the heroes who work
behind the scenes —
thanks and praise I pour.

Our brilliant leaders
have blazed a trail;
the fame of our Folk is growing.

To the serious seekers
for their solitary work
following in Óðinn's footsteps,
who quaff the Mead
and quest for the Runes —
honor and pride I pour.

Always onward,
our efforts continue
to brighten the raven banner;
for the groundwork laid
for a glorious future,
hail to our holy might,
hail to us Heathen Folk!

Fólksdrápa

Fimbultýr's bounty
I bring to the Folk
and honor also
Oðinn's nation.
His holy mead
helps our people
remember well
their mighty spirit.

Our Northern blood
is a noble blessing;
ancestral deeds
have set our doom.
Be it Germanic, Norse,
or mighty English,
through the Well of Wyrd
it works today.

They bore the Runes
and battled Rome;
they conquered lands
and combed the seas.
Through deeds and doings
of daring in the world,
their might and main
have made them famous.

Our ancient ancestors
are an awesome folk.
Our Folk endures
with fame undying.

The roots of our Folk
had run quite deep;
a vicious conversion
they survived intact.
The legacy of language
links us together
across the centuries
of cultural change.

In legend and lore,
their lives we remember
to inspire our spirits
and spur us to act.
Their values and virtues
of vital power
are the holy heritage
of heroes today.

Whether old or new,
ancient or modern:
Our Folk endures
with fame undying.

Our Folk today
has found its roots,
rightly raising
raven banners!
Our ancient gods
we honor again,
bringing their might
back to Midgard.

We learn the lore
and live with virtue;
we rist the Runes
and rown them anew.
We rebuild the bonds
that bind the Folk;
we make it whole
and healthy again.

Our efforts honor
the ancestors well!
Our Folk endures
with fame undying.

With care the Folk
secures its future
and builds a base
— a beacon of hope —
for its work to come
in a world of strife,
for the road ahead
is rough indeed.

Restoring culture
and strengthening kin
will gird our Folk
against its foes.
But act we must
and always struggle
to keep our heritage
secure and whole.

Remember well
this mead I've won
and savor the sweetness
in the sounds I've poured,
for the precious poetry
in potent words
can fortify the Folk
with Fimbultýr's might!

Pagan Praise to Freyr

For Pittsburgh pagans
I pour this mead,
gained from the gladsome Lady.
Gathered together
at this grithful stead,
we honor Ingvi now!

With Freyr today
his fruits we enjoy
and celebrate well the season
while peering forward
and planning the future,
for all in time must end.

Though he's fated to fall
in that future battle
— the infamous Ragnarök —
his fruits and frith
will flourish again
in the realm that's raised anew.

As well for us,
our winters will end,
followed by harvest fruits,
for life anew
is lurking always
beyond the drapes of death.

So here with pride
we praise our Lord,
that great and famous god,
the son of Njörð
and his sister-wife:
the grand and glorious Freyr.

This lord of elves
lives with the Aesir:
a union of tribes through truce.
This god of the Vanir
to Gerð is married:
a union of life and land.

All love Ing
for his excellent boons,
the peace and plenty he brings.
Wide it wanders,
his wagon of blessings,
and now we name his gifts.

For the fruitful fields
and fertile wombs
— the harvests great and good —
we gladly give
our gracious thanks
to the ruler of rain and growth.

For the pleasure and passion
that the people enjoy
— the lust and libido he brings —
we gladly give
our gracious thanks
to the master of phallic might.

For the famous frith
and fortunate weal
— the peace and luck in life —
we gladly give
our gracious thanks
to the god of rightful riches.

In mead with might,
we mix our thanks
and pour that potion to Freyr.
We strengthen the bonds
that bind us together
through a glad exchange of gifts.

Thus may he gift
our great community
for the blessing we bring in frith.
As Pittsburgh Pagans,
we give praise today!
With pride and purpose we hail,
and we hail to fruitful Freyr!

Thor Processional Chant

Great Thor, Thor, Thor,
the thunderer we hail,
that greatest son of Gaut.
We celebrate now
this son of earth
for all his great good gifts.

Ásabrag we hail,
the Aesir lord,
that greatest god of karls.
That warder of workers
gives weal unto all
where oak or rowan rises.

For Man in Midgard
he's a mighty defender
who hallows and holds our shrines.
For Man in Midgard
he's a mainful patron
who furthers the fecund earth.

Eindriði we hail,
and onward he strives
to ward the worlds 'gainst etins.
Gjálp and Greip
and Geirröð, too,
he ended to aid the worlds.

For Man in Midgard
he's a mighty defender
who hallows and holds our shrines.
For Man in Midgard
he's a mainful patron
who furthers the fecund earth.

Harðhugað we hail,
his heart is greatest:
his boldness boosts our courage.
He slew Hrungnir
to hold them safe,
the Bonds and their boons in Asgard.

For Man in Midgard
he's a mighty defender
who hallows and holds our shrines.
For Man in Midgard
he's a mainful patron
who furthers the fecund earth.

Hlórriði we hail
for the help he gives
that blesses our fertile fields.
The rain he brings
in righteous downpours,
by thunder from mighty Mjöllnir.

For Man in Midgard
he's a mighty defender
who hallows and holds our shrines.
For Man in Midgard
he's a mainful patron
who furthers the fecund earth.

Véurr we hail,
that valiant warder
of Midgard's mighty shrines.
Both barrow and vé
he blesses and holds,
hallowing the runes we write.

Hail the hallower
— that holy warder —
hail to Thor, Thor, Thor!
Hail the Great One
— that glorious Ás —
hail to Thor, Thor, Thor!

An Ull Poem

Wulþuz and Wuldor,
as well as Ollerus:
the other names
of Ull we know.
This glorious god
is gifted with skis
and surfs the seas
on a sorcerous bone.

Oaths had Atli
— on Ull's great ring,
sworn to Gunnarr —
forsaken for gold.
The god's blessing
— glory brightest —
departed from him,
replaced by death.

In Ýdalir
is Ull's dwelling,
where winter's winds
are whirling about.
He hunts the game
that happy gods
fix for fine feasts
with fimbul guests.

This accomplished archer
is called upon
— the son of Sif —
for single combat.
Little else we know,
yet lift him a horn
and honor Ull
with excellent mead!

Sumartímadrápa

This song I brewed
with sweetest honey
to celebrate summer
and sun's bright light.
I made this mead
with mirth today,
to fill the folk
with frolic and joy.

Sif and Iðunn
and Sunna we hail
for golden growth
in this greatest time.
Sweet summer is
of seasons best,
with birds and beasts
to brighten the world.

In sun and warmth,
we celebrate life;
the longer days
lift our spirits.
It is greeted as well
by the gods we honor,
for the force of life
is flowing strongest.

For the spirit of life
in this special time,
summer and sunshine
we celebrate now.

The strong sunshine
and storms of summer
will grow the crops
that grace our tables.
The harvest's bounty
is ahead for us:
from brightest light,
the best of food.

The warmth of summer
is welcomed by flowers;
bright and fragrant,
they bloom this season.
Their nourishing nectar
is needed by bees
for the honey made
into heathens' mead.

For the blessings brought
by brighter light,
summer and sunshine
we celebrate now.

Loaded with leaves,
the limbs of trees
provide to us
their valued shade.
To the waters we wend,
in their warmth we swim,
and we take to the roads
for travel and leisure.

For the fun and frolic
of festival days
— the things and moots —
our thanks we give.
We gather to gift
our gods outdoors
with blue sky above
our blessing-steads.

Hail to summer,
that happy season!
Enjoy the sunshine
of these joyful days,
and savor well
the sounds I poured
in the skaldic mead
I skillfully made.

Vetrartímadrápa

I stirred these staves
with strongest honey
to welcome winter
with a wassail now.
I made this mead
with mirth today
to fill the folk
with frolic and joy.

Ull and Skaði
and Óðinn we hail
for wild winter's
wondrous delights.
The winds of winter,
whipping about,
will drive the snows
in this darker time.

The life of the world
now lies in wait,
sleeping soundly
in silent rest.
For the passing away
of the prior year,
winter is greeted
by gods and men.

For the spirit of renewal
in this special time,
winter and wassails
we welcome now.

The Wild Hunt rides,
wending furiously,
with awesome Óðinn
always leading.
In the whistling wind
the unwary are caught;
in rage and wrath
that ride they join.

Inside and safe
we celebrate life
while the restless dead
are roaming the night.
The Hunt is a harvest
that harrows the land,
preparing it well
for the planting to come.

For frights outdoors
and feasts indoors,
winter and wassails
we welcome now.

The Yuletide days
we yearn for most:
those twelve long nights
in our troth are best.
With friends and family
we feast and celebrate,
with flowing mead
and finest meat.

The darkest of days
— when done and past —
brings us the light
we laud and praise.
We gather to gift
our gods by the fire,
warm and happy
with wassail in hand.

Hail to winter,
that hallowed season!
Enjoy the feasting
of these joyful days,
and savor well
the sounds I poured
in the skaldic mead
I skillfully made.

A Yule Poem

Snow is falling,
silently without,
on the ground gleaming
and giving delight.
But the Wild Hunt rides,
wending furiously,
when the cold air
whistles outside.

Snow is falling,
silently without;
the folk meanwhile
are feasting within.
The halls are decked
and the hearth blazes,
showing the spirit
of this special time.

Snow is falling,
silently without;
of sumbel and blót,
celebration begins.
The gods are fained
in this frithful stead;
the might and main
of mead is flowing.

Snow is falling,
silently without;
to gods' folk gathered,
a glad Yule comes.
With waxing light
the wheel has turned,
and holy blessings
are brought to the kin.

Öfundarmál

The towering Tree
is topped by an eagle
who scorns the serpent
for scores of slights.
Haughty, headstrong,
and highfalutin,
that proudest bird
is puffed up well.

Deep in the roots
a dragon lurks,
bitter with bile,
biting corpses.
Sour and surly
(with searing hate
for that damned eagle),
the dragon smolders.

Both up and down,
an acorner runs
along the trunk
of that lofty tree.
He whisks the words
of the wyrm and eagle
both back and forth,
those bitter insults.

Now you may hear
some nuggets of speech
that pass between
those prideful ones,
in reading here thus
the runes of the squirrel;
be wary of finding
that woe within.

The Eagle said:
"Scurry my squirrel,
and scamper quickly;
let that serpent slime
hear slanderous words.
Supreme I am
o'er the piddly snake
because my view
reveals all knowledge."

The Serpent said:
"Scurry my squirrel,
and scamper quickly;
let that 'carry-on' bird
hear accusing words.
I lord o'er realms
that lout can't see;
I simply don't value
the view he has."

The Squirrel said:
"The saw he said
is slander surely,
O wisest wight
of worlds all nine.
That jerk deserves
rejoinders many;
repay his gift
with a prideful 'gild."

And so it goes,
that senseless gab.
Can the hapless hawk
give help at all?
Where is the tree
of this wisdom tale?
Can Elm or Ash
offer assistance?

A Tale of Wisdom's Well

Now wisdom's way I praise
— 'tis Woden's holy road —
with mead I rightly made
from might of lore tonight.
Deeply drink — don't just sip —
this draught of main and gain
in hearing tell of Hár,
on how and why that eye!

First had Búri got Borr.
Then born was Ölvir-Forn:
from a crude corpse he made
what's called our home by skald.
Hanging high, nine nights long,
beholding runes as boons,
this gloried god went far
but glimpsed much more in store.

To get seið-skill he sought
sensuous Freyja then:
ecstasy alters luck.
Through herbs no rot perturbs
the head of Hœnir's bud:
hidden tales it unveils.
They're not enough to quaff:
he needed more of lore.

Wanting to gain he went
for wisdom to be his;
under the Ash he'd wend
by Etin-home and roam
along a root so right
to reach and then beseech
a dram from master Mím:
a mighty trip that sip!

Then grimly Gaut hailed Mím
who, grand with horn in hand,
refused the fuel he prized:
for free it would not be!
A price instead he paid,
a part most dear and near:
to have that gulp he gave
a globe of sight that night.

For gain his eye was gone;
then Gjallarhorn was borne
— deeply undimmed it beamed —
with draught so full of craft.
Crystal clear was its fire;
no clouds stained or remained
in sky of Skollvald's will:
screaming bright, yet no dream.

That member he gave Mím
is mighty still in sight:
rowning of realms unseen,
right it dwells in the wells.
He's stirred to understand
through strength of both at length;
much wisdom deep he draws
from draught and eye of craft.

Onward ever he'll run,
aiming for more to claim
of wisdom wild and bold:
wode for his holy road!
Honor his eye and boon,
for always they recall
that feat of glory great
for Gods and Men to ken.

Yggdrasilsdrápa

From trees are made
us true heathens,
and I seek silence
for singing my praise
of that tallest tree
— truly mighty —
that holds the homes
and is hight Yggdrasil.

From its drops of dew,
a draught I brew
of Ygg's ale now
and open that flow
to stir with words
our wode tonight.
Drink now deeply
this draught of skalds.

Of trees it is best
and I truly name
the nine bright worlds
that needle-ash bears.
The North has Niflheim
and its numbing Ice.
The South has Muspellsheim
and its searing Fire.

The West has Vanaheim,
the world of the Vanir.
The East has Jötunheim,
the Etins' home realm.
Above is Ljósálfheim,
the blessed realm of Elves.
Below is Svartálfheim,
the land of the Dwarves.

Highest is Asgard,
home of the Aesir.
Lowest is Hel,
the land of the Dead.
But Midgard for Man
is in the middle of all.
Now hight are the worlds
that hang on that Tree.

With worlds all nine,
that Wood does shine.
Always that Tree
evergreen shall be.

That Tree rises
from roots and wells;
three each it has,
its thirst they quench.
A root in Hvergelmir
— that roiling cauldron —
provides it the power
of primal nature.

A root in Mímisbrunn
— that Mímir watches —
stores the matter
of memory and wisdom.
A root in Urðarbrunn
— the realm of the Norns —
accumulates the wyrd
that works in the Tree.

From the wells it needs
those waters and deeds.
Always that Tree
evergreen shall be.

Burdened with beasts,
it bears them well.
A stately eagle
stands at the top,
Níðhögg beneath
gnaws on the roots,
and Ratatosk with gossip
runs between them.

Hungry harts four
harrow it also.
Numberless serpents
slither beneath it.
In farthest future
the fire of Surt
will burn the Tree's
trunk and branches.

That harm and thrash
hinders the Ash.
*Though trials arrive,
the Tree will survive.*

Near Urðarbrunn
the Norns do dwell.
The first is Urð
of formative past.
The second is Verðandi
of ceaseless becoming.
The third is Skuld
of threatening due.

With water and mud
they wet the Tree
to keep away
decay and rot,
and they lay layers
for life in the Well;
their faithful work
furthers that Tree.

With wyrd they heal
that Wood's ordeal.
Though trials arrive,
the Tree will survive.

But the best of burdens
it bore of old
when the Aesir's lord
— eager for wisdom —
sought the mysteries
and mounted that Steed
for nights all nine
of needful riding.

Thund was hanging
in thirst and hunger
from high branches
with harrowing wound
to gain by ordeal
a glimpse of death;
thus as gallows
the great Tree served.

The Worker of Wode
wanted the power
that was offered only
by the awesome Runes.
With a final scream
he fulfilled his quest
and lifted at last
their lore from the Tree.

Great Yggdrasil
is always green,
despite the burdens
that would break its spirit;
that source of life
and sacred lore
is ever deserving
of honor and praise.

May Elm and Ash
give ear to these words:
Outside and in,
Yggdrasil is real,
and may this mead
give might to both —
to the Tree without,
to the Tree within!

Rise and Reach the Gods!

O Heathen Folk
in hall and field,
don't grovel to our noble gods.
The Bonds give boons
to the better heathens
as worthiness follows worth.

Óðinn is angered
by acts that are base
and empty of honor and dignity.
Frigg withholds
her favors from bullies,
the craven who shirk all chivalry.

Týr will drop
the driest tears
for folk who refuse to sacrifice.
Thor will turn
his thunderous voice
on cowards who cannot stand.

Freyja has frowns
for the feckless rabble
who lack in love for themselves.
Freyr rejects
ungenerous folk
who need but never give.

O Heathen Folk
in hall and field,
thank our glorious gods,
yet be worthy, wise,
and well-renowned
when you stand and strive for our gods!

Honor Óðinn,
and offer yourself
for his goals and works in the world.
Proclaim and carve
for his cult the Runes;
be worthy of his mighty mead.

Both house and home
keep whole like Frigg,
that exemplar of domestic demeanor.
With keys on your belt,
take care in your duties
for the health of kith and kin.

Trust in Týr,
and seek true selflessness;
put community over your ego.
Remember his hand
and make your sacrifices;
be worthy of the boon of the binding.

Be brave and with heart,
like boldest Thor,
and fight your battles fiercely.
With your stone steady,
stalwart and firm,
you'll be worthy of the valknut's weal.

Be forceful like Freyja
with forthright words;
have zeal for your desires and dignity.
Lead yourself
and love as you will;
be proud and independent!

Follow Freyr,
and seek frith and harvest
in all the deeds you do.
Free your friends
from the fetters that bind;
bring joy and delight to ladies.

*O Heathen Folk
in hall and field,*
such standing is worthy work!
But offer more,
and by aiming higher,
rise and reach the gods!

Earn the Runes
as Óðinn did:
thrive in your thirst and hunger,
ride the Tree,
and then rise again,
waxed in runic wisdom!

Spin like Frigg,
spare not your zeal,
and learn the layers of wyrd!
With wool weave
some weal-filled bonds
to improve your family's future.

Transcend yourself,
as did unswerving Týr,
for the power that binds great bale.
With a self that's serene,
reach the center,
the pole that offers order.

Through strength be holy,
like strongest Thor
who shines with self-assurance.
Seek the secrets
of his sacred hammer
to give the gift of life.

Face the flames,
as Freyja did,
and seek a bright rebirth!
From Gullveig to Heið,
she gained in power;
transform and fulfill your wyrd!

Be giving at heart,
like gladsome Freyr,
to know the finest frith
which grows the crops
and grows the kindreds;
through gifting, gain aplenty.

*O Heathen Folk
in hall and field,*
rightly stand or rise,
for the Ragnarök
is really coming,
though far in the future it seems.

Whether you stand
and strive with work
or rise and reach the gods,
on that darkest day,
there are deeds awaiting
you and the best that you bring!

But the future aside,
there's a fight today,
so aid the Aesir now!
Pride you may take
for your place in it,
but only if you stand and strive,
or only if you rise and reach!

www.ingramcontent.com/pod-product-compliance
Lightning Source LLC
Chambersburg PA
CBHW020128130526
44591CB00032B/572